]

H(

The

F

ILLUSTRATED BY
ED BOXALL

For pupils and staff at Dallington CEP School, East Sussex,
where I am their Patron of Reading

Published by TROIKA
First published 2018

Troika Books Ltd
Well House, Green Lane, Ardleigh CO7 7PD, UK
www.troikabooks.com

Text copyright © Brian Moses 2018
Illustrations copyright © Ed Boxall 2018
The moral rights of the author and illustrator have been asserted

A CIP catalogue record for this book is available
from the British Library

ISBN 978-1-909991-74-3

1 2 3 4 5 6 7 8 9 10

Printed in Poland

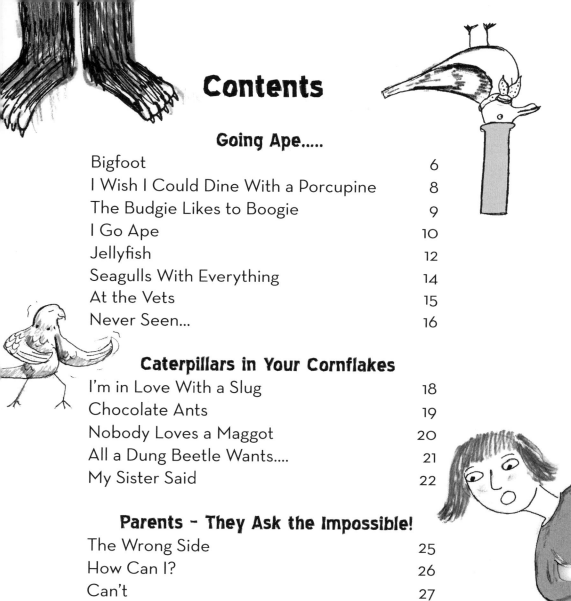

Contents

Going Ape.....

Caterpillars in Your Cornflakes

Parents - They Ask the Impossible!

No Brother of Mine.....or Sister

Every Boy and Every Girl Need Wriggle Room

In Some Distant Magical Place

Bigfoot

Our house is full of Bigfoot
or should that be Bigfeet?
We watched them from our window
as they stumbled down the street.

They knocked upon our door
and asked to come inside.
'Don't leave us here,' they pleaded,
'We need a place to hide.'

Now there's Bigfeet in the kitchen
and Biggerfeet in the hall.
On a patch of grass in our garden,
Bigfeet are playing football.

There's Bigfeet in our garage
and Bigfeet in the shed,
while underneath the duvet,
Bigfeet sleep in my bed.

Bigfeet lounge in the lounge
all watching our TV.
There's nowhere much to sit
since they've broken our settee.

Some Bigfoot put his foot
right through our bedroom ceiling.
The darkness in our loft, he said,
was really quite appealing.

The airing cupboard Bigfoot
keeps our water hot.
'No problem at all,' he says,
I like this job a lot.'

They make an awful racket
up and down our stairs,
they queue to use the bathroom
and block the sink with hairs.

At night they growl and snore,
loud as a thunderstorm,
but all these fur coats everywhere
keep us cosy and warm!

7

I Wish I Could Dine
With a Porcupine

I wish I could dine with a porcupine
or take afternoon tea with a whale.
I wish I could race with a cheetah
or visit the house of a snail.

I wish I could chat with a bat
and learn about its habits.
I wish I could dig a deep burrow
and spend the day with rabbits.

I wish I could fly balloons with baboons
or watch jellyfish eating jelly.
I wish I could perfume spray a skunk
so he wouldn't be quite so smelly.

I wish I could learn about a worm
as I slide along on my tummy,
or meet a baby hippo
and his hippopotamummy.

I wish I could feast with a wildebeast
or rescue a mule from his load.
I wish I could bake a cake with a snake
or hop down the road with a toad.

I wish I could take all these creatures
for a holiday by the sea,
we'd have our own beach barbecue
and toast marshmallows for tea.

The Budgie likes to Boogie

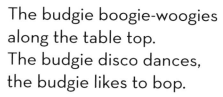

The budgie likes to boogie,
the budgie likes to rock.
He wakes us every night
when he rocks around the clock.

The budgie likes to jive,
to spin around, to twirl.
His body full of rhythm,
his head is in a whirl.

The budgie boogie-woogies
along the table top.
The budgie disco dances,
the budgie likes to bop.

He's just about the best
and his moves are really neat.
You should see the budgie boogie,
you should see his flying feet!

In front of the dangly mirror
he plays his air guitar.
The budgie likes to boogie,
the budgie is a STAR!

9

I Go Ape

When I hang upside down, I'm orang-utang,
when I climb a tree, I'm chimpanzee,
when I'm tough as Attila, you can call me gorilla,
but to keep in shape, I go ape.

I go, I go, I go ape, I go, I go, I go ape.

oo oo oo oo oo oo oo!

I'm with people of every size and shape
looking for adventure and going ape,
leaving the streets and leaving the town
for the joys of hanging upside down.

I wanna let all my energy escape,
like a marathon runner reaching the tape,
show everybody how fit I can be,
I wanna release the hidden monkey in me
and go ape.

I go, I go, I go ape, I go, I go, I go ape.

oo oo oo oo oo oo oo!

If there's no pain, there can be no gain,
maybe I could be Tarzan, you could be Jane,
swinging so high we could hang from the stars,
slide Saturn's rings and cartwheel on Mars.

When I hang upside down, I'm orang-utang,
when I climb a tree, I'm chimpanzee,
when I'm tough as Attila, you can call me gorilla,
but to keep in shape, I go ape.

I go, I go, I go ape, I go, I go, I go ape.

oo oo oo oo oo oo oo!

Jellyfish

Jellyfish,
jellyfish,
floats along and slaps you on the belly
fish.

Just when you thought you'd go for a swim,
just when you thought it was safe to go in.

Jellyfish,
jellyfish,
saw one in a programme on the telly
fish.

Thinking about it kept me awake,
I just don't think that I can take

Jellyfish,
jellyfish,
trod on one at Margate with Aunt Nelly
fish

If you see one in the sea then give me a shout,
catch it in a bucket but keep your fingers out.

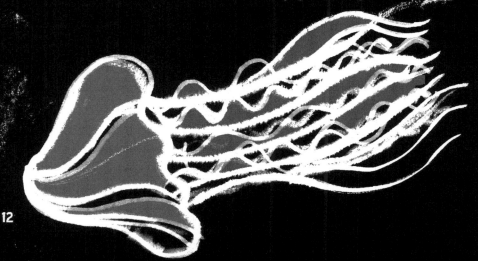

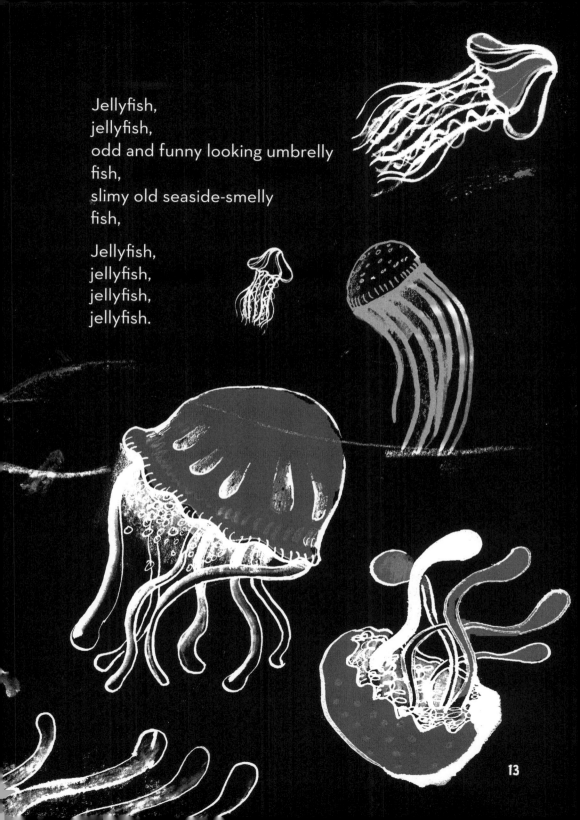

Jellyfish,
jellyfish,
odd and funny looking umbrelly
fish,
slimy old seaside-smelly
fish,

Jellyfish,
jellyfish,
jellyfish,
jellyfish.

Seagulls With Everything

You get seagulls with everything
at St. Ives......

Seagulls with walking sticks,
seagulls with glasses,
seagulls with lipstick
and ones with moustaches.

Seagulls with hats
to cover bald heads,
seagulls with duvets
still lying in bed.

Seagulls with tickets
to travel on trains,
seagulls with telescopes
high up on cranes.

Seagulls with lollies
and ice cream cones,
seagulls with diaries
and mobile phones.

Seagulls in shades
strumming guitars,
seagulls with girlfriends
driving fast cars.

Seagulls with dreams
to fly from St. Ives
and be big movie stars
for the rest of their lives.

At the Vets

When we took our dog to the vets
we sat and waited with all kinds of pets.

There were hamsters with headaches
and fish with the flu,
there were rats and bats
and a lame kangaroo.

There were porcupines
with spines that were bent
and a poodle that must have been
sprinkled with scent.

There were dogs that were feeling
terribly grumpy
and monkeys with mumps looking
awfully lumpy.

There were rabbits with rashes
and foxes with fleas,
there were thin mice in need of
a large wedge of cheese.

There were cats complaining
of painful sore throats,
there were gerbils and geese
and two travel sick goats.

There were two chimpanzees
who both had toothache,
and the thought of the vet
made everyone S H A K E.....

15

Never Seen...

Never seen a hyena with a vacuum cleaner,
never seen a goat in a boat.
Never seen a pike on a motorbike
but I've seen an anaconda in a Honda.

Never seen a fish in a satellite dish,
never seen a whale in the Royal Mail.
Never seen a llama unpeel a banana
but I've seen an anaconda in a Honda.

Never seen a tadpole do a forward roll,
never seen a frog weightlifting a log.
Never seen a poodle cooking noodles
but I've seen an anaconda in a Honda.

Never seen a panda in an armoured tank,
never seen a tortoise at a taxi rank.
Never seen a tiger rob a national bank
but I've seen an anaconda in a Honda

And I've watched him
  wander
          and weave
      all
          over
    the road.

Caterpillars in Your Cornflakes.......

I'm in Love with a Slug

I'm in love with a slug,
I really think she's neat,
right from the eyes in her antennae
down to the tips of her feet.**

Yes, I'm in love with a slug,
we meet up every night,
while she's feeding in the lettuces
I watch each tender bite.

I hold her in my hand
as she looks at me with affection.
My heart begins to sing
when faced with such perfection.

If I could shrink to her size
I'd accompany her as she dines.
I'd like to toast her beauty
in a range of dandelion wines.

And I know I'd be the slug
she'd fall in love with too,
and underneath the slippery moon
we'd kiss, the way slugs do.

*** Actually slugs only have one 'foot'
but I needed 'feet' for the rhyme!*

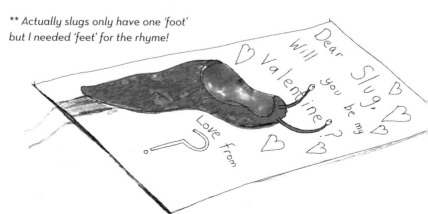

Chocolate Ants

If they started to sell
chocolate-covered ants
at the superstore
would you buy them?

If they gave them away
in a tasting test
would you buy one?

If they said these are yummy,
and good for you too,
they keep away colds
and protect you from flu,

would you say
you can give me
a packet or two?

And if you liked them
maybe you'd try....

aniseed fleas
and jelly slugs,
suger-coated earwigs
or peppermint bugs.

A range of tastes
just waiting for you,
try 'Eleph-ants'
for a jumbo chew.

But I'd say no way-
I just couldn't,
could you?

yeuch!
Don't
do it!

Nobody Loves a Maggot

Nobody wants to tickle
a maggot under its chin.
Nobody yells, 'Hooray,'
I've got maggots in my bin.

Nobody whispers secrets
into a maggot's ear.
Nobody says, 'Get the party started
now that the maggot's here.'

Maggots are shunned, unspoken of
and generally ignored.
Nothing much for maggots to do
so they probably get bored.

They don't feature on television,
they're never heroes in a book.
A maggot's public appearance
is pinned to a fishing hook.

Like nature's other irritants,
wasps and slugs and fleas,
nobody loves a maggot
or wants to give one a squeeze.

A maggot is not a special guest,
not someone to welcome in.
A maggot's place can only be
inside a smelly bin.

All a Dung Beetle Wants....

It's no good offering a dung beetle
fish and chips,
it won't make him lick his lips.
It's no good serving him ice cream,
you won't hear a delighted scream.
He won't be in a hurry
to find himself a curry.
He won't take the quickest route
to buy some tasty fruit.
He'll never think it a treat
to have something sweet to eat.
He won't ever fill his belly
with sticky strawberry jelly.
He won't lift the lid of the cookie jar
or be first in line at the burger bar.
He won't say please
for a hunk of cheese,
or pay good money
for a tub of honey.
He doesn't like foods
that please me and you.
All a dung beetle wants
is a big lump of.....
POO!

My Sister Said

My sister said,
'If you do that to me again,
I'll put.....

Slugs in your shoes,
spiders in your vest,
earwigs in your ear
and caterpillars in your cornflakes.

I'll put....
Beetles between your sheets.
squirmy worms in your hair,
centipedes in your lunchbox
and grasshoppers, (real whoppers) in
your slippers.

I'll put....
ants in your knickers,
woodlice under your pillow,
snails in your school bag
and nits in your nightwear.'

'I'll really make you scream,' she said,
'You'll yell and shake and shiver......'

And I know that she will,
and I promise I won't........NOT EVER!.

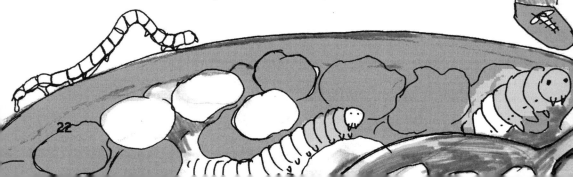

22

Parents - they ask the impossible!

The Wrong Side

My mother used to tell me
I'd got out of bed
on the wrong side, which was strange
as there was only one side
I could tumble from.

The other was hard against the wall
and all I did was bang
my knee, but still she insisted
that she was right.

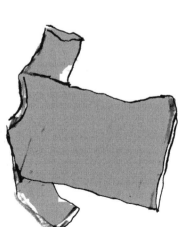

So one bright morning
I tried it out, squeezed
between the wall and my bed,
then said nothing.
She never knew, I was puzzled.

My mother said how she'd teach me
to choose between wrong and right,
but if I got out the right side
and that was wrong,
then who was right?

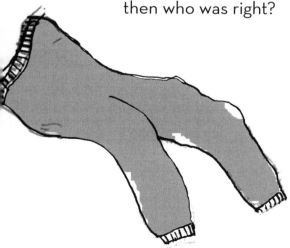

How Can I?

How can I wind up my brother
when I haven't got the key?

How can I turn on my charm
when I can't even find the switch?

How can I snap at my mother
when I'm not a crocodile?

How can I stir up my sister
when I'm not even holding a spoon?

How can I pick up my feet
and not fall to the ground on my knees?

How can I stretch my legs
when they're long enough already?

Parents! – They ask the impossible!

Can't

My mum used to say,
take the 't' out of 'can't' and you 'can'.
Or sometimes' she'd say,
'There's no such word as can't.'
But I've found things I can't do.....

I can't lick my nose with my tongue,
I can't bite my toenails,
I can't give the kiss of life to a dead beetle,
I can't scratch my ear with my foot
like my dog can,
I can't keep money in my piggy bank
without spending it,
I can't do the splits like my sister can,
I can't predict
what my football team will do at the weekend.
(They sometimes surprise me, mostly dismay me!)

Take the 't' out of 'can't' and you 'can'
    my mum said.
        But I've got news for her,
           however hard I try,
             however hard I want to believe her,
                there are still some things I just can't do.

Christmas Eve

I'm trying to sleep on Christmas Eve
but I really can't settle down,
and I don't want to lie
with wide open eyes
till the morning comes around.

I hear Mum and Dad downstairs,
doing their best to keep quiet,
and although I'm in bed
with my favourite ted,
in my head there's a terrible riot.

I'm thinking of Christmas morning
and all the presents I'll find,
but what if I've missed
something good off my list,
it keeps going round in my mind.

Mum has been baking all day
making rolls, mince pies and cake,
and I know quite well
it's this heavenly smell
that's keeping me wide awake.

Perhaps I'll slip down for some water
though I ought to stay in my room,
but maybe I'll risk
a slap with the whisk
for a lick of Mum's mixing spoon.

If I had just one mince pie
then I know it would be alright,
fast asleep,
not another peep,
my eyes shut tightly all night.

Now Dad says Father Christmas
won't leave any presents for me,
Make no mistake,
if you're still awake,
he'll pass you by, you'll see!

But I've tried and I've tried and I've tried
and I keep rolling round in my bed,
I still can't sleep,
and I'm fed up with sheep
so I'm counting reindeer instead!

Puzzle

I thought I was the biggest child
in our little family,
but Mum says Dad's the biggest child
so where does that leave me?

It Isn't Raining on My Side of the Car

It isn't raining on my side of the car,
and I don't want to sit inside now we've travelled this far.
Please let me out, unlock the door,
there's a whole new beach for me to explore,
and it isn't raining on my side of the car.

On the side I'm on the sky is turning blue,
I can see a rainbow, the sun is shining through.
Let's go outside and start to play,
we've already wasted half the day,
and it isn't raining on my side of the car.

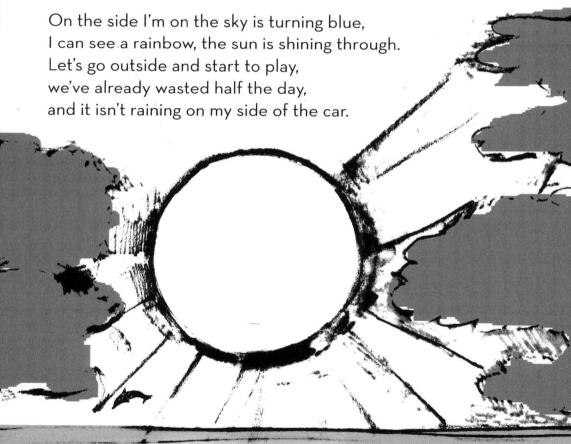

It's Not the Same Without Dad

I always sat on his knee
for the scary bits when we watched TV,
my head tucked into his chest,
Mum always fidgets, Dad was best

And it's not the same without Dad.

He piggy-backed me up the stairs,
pulled sticky bubblegum out of my hair,
didn't tell Mum when he should have done
when Dad played around it was really fun.

And it's not the same without Dad.

We fed the ducks down at the park,
he held me when I was scared of the dark
he didn't mind if I got things wrong,
when I felt weak, he was sure to be strong.

But everything's changed now he's gone.

Up a Tree

Look at us now, we're stuck up a tree,
me, my big sister and Kevin who's three,
not knowing whether to risk going down,
grey sky up above and leaves all around.

We're stuck up a tree one Sunday in June
hoping that someone comes past very soon.
I bet that we've missed something good on TV,
I wish we'd chosen an easier tree.

'I bet you can't climb it,' some big lad laughed,
and none of us likes to look feeble or daft
so we tried, and we've climbed up far too high,
and I know, very soon, Kevin's going to cry.

And big sisters's frozen herself to the tree,
I think she's forgotten our Kevin and me,
she's moaning softly and won't look down
and it seems like a very long drop to the ground.

Soon someone must surely pass by this tree,
some afternoon walker who'll look up and see
three frightened kids clinging desperately,
me, my big sister, and Kevin who's three.

The Fairies Must Have Taken My Brother

The fairies must have taken my brother,
swapped him soon after he was born,
left us some wriggly nasty thing
that screams from sundown till dawn.

He laughs when things go wrong
and yells when everything's fine.
He grabs all the food from the table
and steals what's left of mine.

He's an impish creature, with a face
that twists to a horrid shape.
His voice is a devilish babble
and it's something we can't escape.

But my parents don't seem concerned
when I say what the fairies have done.
They beam at him and smile
and never notice what he's become.

When he isn't screaming and bawling
you can hear him whimper and whine.
Yes, the fairies have taken my brother
and what's left is no brother of mine.

Are We Nearly There Yet?

When we went on holiday this year
my little sister just wouldn't be quiet.

Again and again
she kept on asking,
'Are we nearly there yet?'

We drove to the end of our street
and my sister said,
'Are we nearly there yet?'

We left the town behind
and again she said,
'Are we nearly there yet?'

We stopped for a train to go by
and my sister called,
'Are we nearly there yet?'

We sped along the motorway
and my sister said,
'Are we nearly there yet?'

We stopped for something to eat
and my sister grumbled,
'Are we nearly there yet?'

We waited in a queue of cars
and my sister screamed.
'Are we nearly there there?'

We caught a glimpse of the sea
and my sister yawned,
'Are we nearly there yet?'

But when we finally reached the end
of our long and tiring trip,

my sister didn't say anything,
she was fast asleep....zzzZZZZZZ!

The GGGGGGGGhost Train

On the g-g-g-g-g-g-g-g-ghost train,
it was dark, it was scary, it was insane,
and I'm never going back there ever again
on the g-g-g-g-g-g-g-g-ghost train.

'It's a lot of fun,' my big sister said,
'skeletons, ghosts and a man with his head
tucked under his arm, but you needn't look,
I've been here before.' So I sat and I shook

On the g-g-g-g-g-g-g-g-ghost train.

I didn't like it, not one bit,
webs hung down from the ceiling and hit
the side of my face as we travelled past
ever so slowly- oh can't we go fast? –

On the g-g-g-g-g-g-g-g-ghost train.

AAAAAH!

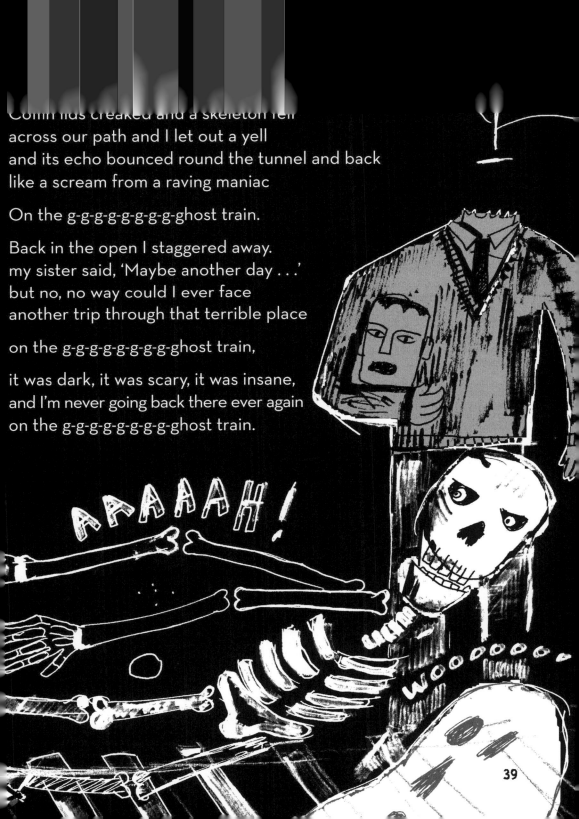

Coffin lids creaked and a skeleton fell
across our path and I let out a yell
and its echo bounced round the tunnel and back
like a scream from a raving maniac

On the g-g-g-g-g-g-g-g-ghost train.

Back in the open I staggered away.
my sister said, 'Maybe another day . . .'
but no, no way could I ever face
another trip through that terrible place

on the g-g-g-g-g-g-g-g-ghost train,

it was dark, it was scary, it was insane,
and I'm never going back there ever again
on the g-g-g-g-g-g-g-g-ghost train.

AAAAAH!

WOOOOOO

Face Pulling Contests

My sister and I
hold face pulling contests.

I start with my
zombie at midnight look
while she hooks two fingers
into her mouth and pulls out
her sabre tooth tiger scowl.

I try my curse
of the killer mummies,
but she rolls her eyes
and curls her lip,
sticks out her teeth
and pretends she's Drac.
I clutch at my throat
and finger a bolt,
then zap her with
Frankenstein's features.

She comes at me
with her wolf woman sneer,
but I can howl
much better than her.
And now she's stuck
for something to do,
and this time I'm thinking
I'll beat her for sure
with my purple planet people eater...

when Mum steps in
to check the noise,
and no one pulls a better face
than Mum when she's annoyed.

My sister and I
are mere beginners:

Mum's the winner!

This Time

I'm always doing things wrong,
I never get them right.
My sister always laughs
and that's when we start to fight.
We wrestle in the living room,
I chase her up the stairs,
she flings the door in my face
and I ROAR like an angry bear.

Inside her room she's hiding
but I know just where she'll be,
crouched inside her wardrobe
waiting to jump out on me.
Then Dad calls out, 'If you can't behave,
I've told you what we'll do,
we'll go away for a holiday
and we won't be taking you.
Your Mum and I are tired
of your squabbles around the home,
if we leave you here together,
you'll have to get by on your own.'

My sister comes out of the wardrobe
and we kneel by the bedroom door:
'Do you think they really mean it?'
'I don't know, I couldn't be sure.'

'If you think we don't really mean it,'
Dad shouts, 'then just you step out of line.'
We look at each other, both thinking the same,
they really must mean it, this time!

Every boy and
every girl need
wriggle room......

44

Problems

A voice was saying on Breakfast TV
how we really should be taking more care
of our planet; and I thought between bites
of toast and jam, how it really must
get untidy sometimes. I wondered
if God ever shouted out loud,
like Mum when my room's in a dreadful state:
Hey you lot, isn't it about time
you set to work and tidied your planet?
Then another voice said, this world
is sick, and I wondered how he knew.
You could hardly feel its nose
like a dog, or shove a thermometer
under its tongue. Such problems were
far too complicated and I needed
expert advice, but my teacher
didn't know when I asked and joked
that she only knew where to look when
answers came out of a book. She told me
instead, that my maths was a mess
and my handwriting wasn't tidy.
She didn't seem to understand,
I had far bigger problems on my mind.

Lost Property Box

In our lost property box
there are socks with holes in
and shoes minus laces,
stand-up figures
without any bases,
a faded T-shirt
from Lanzarotte,
a greatest hits tape
by Pavarotti,
once champion conkers
shrunken with age,
a mystery book
without the last page,
sandwich boxes
with last month's bread in,
P.E. shorts,
I wouldn't be seen dead in,
unloved toys and
mislaid gloves,
a Christmas card with
two turtle doves,
red underpants
decidedly manky,
a barely used
lace-edged hanky,
a love letter
from David Pratt
to his girlfriend Sally,
what about that!

And right at the bottom,
what I'm looking for,
the sports shirt I borrowed
from the boy next door...

Perhaps he'll speak to me again
now I've found it!

LOST PROPERTY

The Overtaker

I'm an overtaker,
off down the line.
I don't wait around
I haven't got time.

I'm an overtaker,
I can't stay back,
I'm out in front
ahead of the pack.

Better keep clear
in the swimming bath.
Everybody
out of my path.

I'm an overtaker,
watch me run,
every sports day,
sound of the gun.

There I go,
off down the track,
nothing is going
to hold me back.

Head in the clouds,
I don't look round,
keep my feet
clear of the ground.

Run to school,
everyday,
any old race,
I'm okay.

Dash home at night,
have lots of fun.
I'm an overtaker,
watch me r.................un!

Wriggle Room

When it's assembly time
and you're sitting in line,
what do you need,
you need wriggle room.

When it's a bit of a strain
on a railway train,
what do you need,
you need wriggle room.

When you're tucked up in bed
with your favourite ted,
what do you need,
you need wriggle room.

When you're travelling far
in the back of a car,
what do you need,
you need wriggle room.

All the penguins in the zoo
need wriggle room.
A baby kangaroo
needs wriggle room.

All the angels in Heaven
need wriggle room.
Man U first eleven
need wriggle room.

All the motorway cars
need wriggle room.
The moon and the stars
need wriggle room.

Frogs on a log
need wriggle room.
Fleas on a dog
need wriggle room.

Every boy & every girl
needs wriggle room.
In an overcrowded world
what do we need?

WRIGGLE ROOM!

Wriggle room,
wriggle room,
wriggle room,
wriggle room.

What do we need?
We need
wriggle room!

Sounds

Miss asked if we had any favourite sounds,
and could we quickly write them down.
Tim said the screeeeam of a mean guitar
or a saxophone or a fast sports car.
Shakira said cats when they purr on your lap,
and Jamie, the CRASH of a thunderclap.
Paul asked what word he could possibly write
for the sound of a rocket on Guy Fawkes Night,
or a redwood tree as it fell to the ground
and Miss said to write it as it sounds.
So Paul wrote wooooooooooooosh with a dozen 'o's
and CRACK with a crack in it, just to show
the kind of noise a tree might make
as it hit the ground and made it SHAKE
Then everyone began to call, hey listen to this,
what do you think? Or is this right Miss,
I can't decide, if balloons go POP or BANG
or BUST, or do bells peeeeal or just CLANG
Then Miss said it was quite enough
and time to stop all the silly stuff.
What she really likes, as she's often said,
is a quiet room, with every head
bent over books, writing things down.
The sound of silence, her favourite sound!

Peasy!

You want me to do that ten figure sum,
                              that's peasy!

Wind my legs over that bar,
slide down into a forward roll
with a double back flip to follow.
                              Huh, peasy!

Build a working model of Big Ben
from Technical Lego,
                              Oh that's peasy!

Clear that five foot hurdle in one leap,
cross country run up a mountain peak,
keep writing a story for one whole week,
                              peasy!

Score thirty goals in record time,
in ten minutes write a thousand lines,
say 'Supercalifragilisticexpialidocious'
two hundred times, backwards!
                              Oh that's all far too peasy!

BUT.....

Eat the skin off of custard.
Ugh! That's the toughest thing in the world!

Don't Be Such a Fusspot

Don't be such a fusspot,
an always-in-a-rushpot.

Don't be such a weepypot
a sneak-to-mum-and-be-creepypot.

Don't be such a muddlepot,
a double-dose-of-troublepot.

Don't be such a wigglepot,
a sit-on-your-seat-don't-squigglepot.

Don't be such a muckypot,
a pick-up-slugs-and-be-yuckypot.

Don't be such a sleepypot,
a beneath-the-bedclothes-peepypot.

Don't be such a fiddlepot,
a mess-about-and-meddlepot.

Don't be such a bossypot,
a saucypot, a gigglepot,

Don't be such a lazypot,
a nigglepot, a slackpot.

And don't call me a crackpot...
Who do you think you are?

Glitterbread

I'm so bored with pitta bread
I want glitterbread.

Bread that gleams when it catches the light,
bread that glows like the stars at night,

Bread that sparkles then starts to shimmer,
bread that dazzles and never grows dimmer,

Bread that lights my way back home,
bread that shines like a precious stone

I want glitterbread all the time,
something unique, totally mine.

Ellie's Smelly Wellies

(Apparently you can actually buy wellington boots that smell of strawberries!)

Everyone wanted to smell
Ellie's smelly wellies.

Rose said they smelt of roses.

Lily said definitely lilies.

India caught a whiff
of curry.

Rosemary said rosemary,
with maybe some parsley and thyme.

Lavender said lavender.

Primrose caught the scent of spring
and Blossom did too.

Only Hermione, who didn't like Ellie,
said that Ellie's wellies
smelt of cow poo!

But Ellie didn't care.

When she squeezed her toes
deep into her wellies she smelt

cut grass,
Spanish oranges,
sea breezes,
strawberry teas

and only the very slightest trace

of cowpat.

Freepost Elephant

I saw a van that said *Freepost Elephant*
and I thought that must be
the biggest bargain you could get.
Imagine how much it would normally cost
to post an elephant,
think of all the paper you'd need
to wrap it up,
all the sellotape or string.
And where would you write the address?

Hard luck for the postman.
He'd need a special truck to deliver it,
reinforced, steel plated.
And of course, anyone who took delivery
of such a parcel would need
a jumbo sized door.

Maybe the same firm would have other offers:
Freepost Jaguar, our fastest service ever.
Freepost Crocodile – making it snappy!

Freepost Elephant sounds like a bargain
but who on earth would need it?
Who'd be daft enough to send
an elephant through the post?

Freepost Elephant.
That's something big
to think about today.

IS IT A PUPPY?

THIS WAY UP

TO
SAMUEL BOXALL
CHIEF ZOO KEEPER
WOLF TOWN ZOO
FREEPOST 71429

FRAGILE

Into the Lair of Baron Jugula

No light ever falls on the bushes and trees,
the flowers there are mostly diseased,
but I went there once for a dare.
I went into the lair of Baron Jugula,
past brambles that tore at my face,
past skulls, picked clean and grinning,
past savage hounds that bayed at my heels,
past the coils of a sleeping three headed snake,
past monstrous eyes and fearsome fangs,
right up to the door of Baron Jugula's Castle
where I stopped and knocked.

And the door swung open to reveal
the bloated, loathsome face
of Baron Jugula.
His breath stank and I shrank back
then remembered why I'd come:
'Can I have my ball back please?'

I Thought I Heard a Tree Sneeze

I thought I heard a tree sneeze.
I'm not really surprised,
standing out there in all weathers,
damp feet, a cloak of wet leaves,
is it any wonder they catch cold?

I wouldn't be pleased
to be a tree, couldn't nip out
for cough sweets or a quick vapour rub
down my bark.
I'd be left all night in the dark,
feeling shivery, feeling cold.

I thought I heard a tree sneeze,
but perhaps I was mistaken.

What do you think?

One Shoe

One shoe by the roadside,
who on earth is careless enough
to lose one shoe?
Surely you'd notice if you hobbled home
on one shoe?
Surely you'd think it was odd?
Some do gooder would shout out -
'Where's your other shoe then?'
Some busybody would comment -
'That's a strange way to walk!'
You'd be the talk of the town,
one shoe off, one on,
one foot up, one down.
And how could you ever replace
your lost shoe?
Have you ever tried going into a shoe shop
and saying, 'I'll just take one please.'
Shoes come in pairs, like socks,
you don't find one shoe shops.
So if you're careless and lose one shoe,
best lose the other one too.

Lost Kite

Our kite was a magic bird
and the wind took it into the sky,
above our heads, above the trees,
flying way up high.

But the wind was a thief
who wanted our kite,
it tugged and tugged
with all its might.

And the wind was a blade
that could cut anything,
it took our kite
and left us the string.

We watched it twist and dive
we heard it flutter and swish.
We felt it flap and fall
and wriggle like a fish.

Then it took our kite again
and raced it up a hill,
it tied the string around
the sails of an old windmill.

Our kite was caught again
in the branches of a tree.
but the wind blew long and hard
until the kite broke free.

We watched it twist and dive
we heard it flutter and swish.
We felt it flap and fall
and wriggle like a fish.

Next it found a church
and twisted round the spire,
then flipped across the street
to hook on telephone wire.

Then the wind gave a mighty gust
and we lost sight of our kite,
we were looking for it everywhere
while the day was losing its light.

And as we stared from our window
to see the face of the moon,
we wondered if our kite
might be passing by there soon.

We watched it twist, we watched it dive,
we heard it flutter and swish.
We watched it flap and fall
and wriggle like a fish.

And we both remember that kite,
we know we always will.
In some distant magical place
it's sure to be flying still.

About the Author

BRIAN MOSES has been a professional children's poet since 1988. He has had over 200 books published including *Lost Magic* and *The Monster Sale* and edited anthologies such as *The Secret Lives of Teachers* and *Aliens Stole My Underpants.* Brian also runs writing workshops and performs his own poetry and percussion shows. He has given over 3000 performances in schools, libraries, theatres and at festivals in UK and abroad. Brian is co-director of a nationwide able writers' scheme administered by Authors Abroad.

To find out more about Brian visit his website www.brianmoses.co.uk

About the Illustrator

ED BOXALL is a childrens' poet, illustrator, musician, educator and performer. He has written and illustrated many books, such as *Mr Trim and Miss Jumble* for Walker Books and *High In The Old Oak Tree* for his own Pearbox Press. Ed performs his poems with a mix of spoken word, projections at schools, art centres and festivals. He lives in Hastings, a small town on the south coast of England.

To find out more about Ed visit his website www.edboxall.com